Maths — No Problem!

Singapore Maths
English National Curriculum 2014

Consultant and Author
Dr. Yeap Ban Har

UK Consultant
Dr. Anne Hermanson

Authors
Dr. Foong Pui Yee
Chang Suo Hui
Lim Li Gek Pearlyn
Wong Oon Hua

shinglee

Published by Maths — No Problem!
Copyright © 2017 by Maths — No Problem!

Printed in the United Kingdom
First Printing, 2015
Reprinted twice in 2015, once in 2016 and once in 2017

ISBN 978-1-910504-06-2

Maths — No Problem!
Dowding House, Coach & Horses Passage
Tunbridge Wells, UK TN2 5NP
www.mathsnoproblem.co.uk

Acknowledgements

This Maths — No Problem! series, adapted from the New Syllabus
Primary Mathematics series, is published in collaboration with
Shing Lee Publishers. Pte Ltd.

Design and Illustration by Kin

Preface

Maths — No Problem! is a comprehensive series that adopts a spiral design with carefully built-up mathematical concepts and processes adapted from the maths mastery approaches used in Singapore. The Concrete-Pictorial-Abstract (C-P-A) approach forms an integral part of the learning process through the materials developed for this series.

Maths — No Problem! incorporates the use of concrete aids and manipulatives, problem-solving and group work.

In Maths — No Problem! Primary 1, these features are exemplified throughout the chapters:

Chapter Opener

Familiar events or occurrences that serve as an introduction for pupils.

In Focus

Includes questions related to various lesson objectives as an introductory activity for pupils.

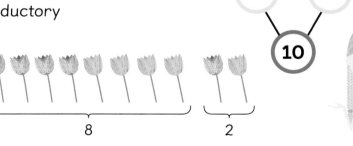

Let's Learn

Introduces new concepts through a C-P-A approach with the use of engaging pictures and manipulatives. Guided examples are provided for reinforcement.

Activity Time

Provides pupils with opportunities to work as individuals or in small groups to explore mathematical concepts or to play games.

Guided Practice

Comprises questions for further consolidation and for the immediate evaluation of pupils' learning.

Mind Workout

Challenging non-routine questions for pupils to apply relevant heuristics and to develop higher-order thinking skills.

Maths Journal

Provides pupils with opportunities to show their understanding of the mathematical concepts learnt.

Self Check

Allows pupils to assess their own learning after each chapter.

I know how to...

☐ solve word problems involving addition or subtraction.

Contents

How many stepping stones are there?

Chapter 10
Numbers to 40

Counting to 40

In Focus

How many stepping stones are there altogether?

Let's Learn

1 We can use cubes to make tens and count.

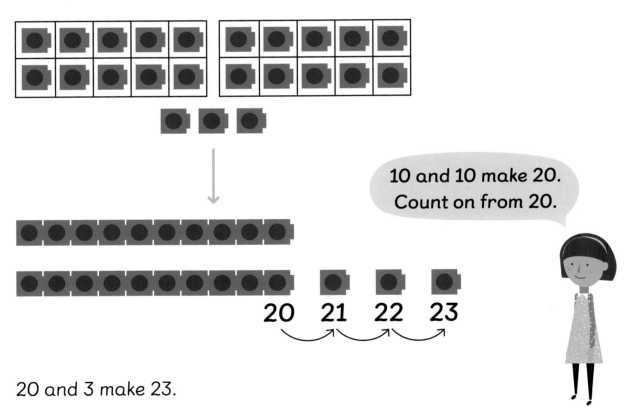

10 and 10 make 20.
Count on from 20.

20 21 22 23

20 and 3 make 23.

2 How many beads are there?

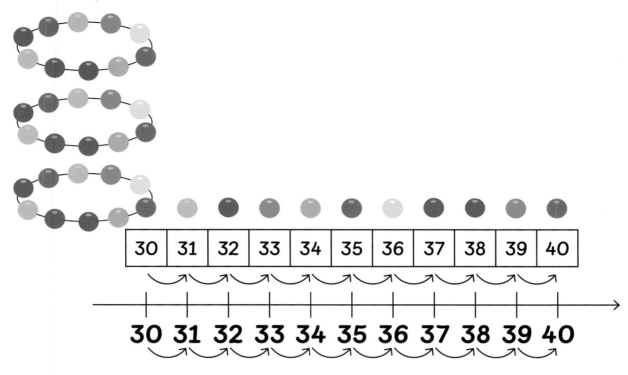

| 30 | 31 | 32 | 33 | 34 | 35 | 36 | 37 | 38 | 39 | 40 |

30 31 32 33 34 35 36 37 38 39 40

There are 40 beads.

Work in pairs.

What you need:

① Take more than 20 but fewer than 40 cubes.

② Ask your partner to count the number of by making tens.

③ Take turns to repeat ① and ②.

21

Guided Practice

1 Count in tens and ones.

Show the number on the number chart.

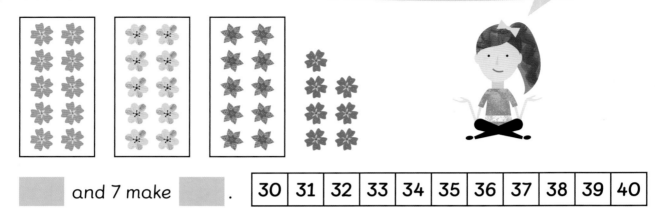

| | | and 7 make | | . | 30 | 31 | 32 | 33 | 34 | 35 | 36 | 37 | 38 | 39 | 40 |

2 Count in tens and ones.

30 and ☐ make ☐ .

Show the number on the number line.

| | | | | | | | | |
30 31 32 33 34 35 36 37 38

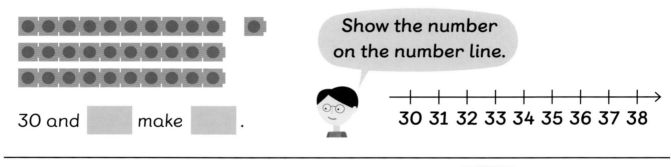

☐ and ☐ make ☐ .

Show the number on the number line.

20 21 22 23 24 25 26 27 28

☐ and ☐ make ☐ .

Show the number on the number line.

0   10   20   30   40

Complete Worksheet 1 – Page 1 – 4

Writing Numbers to 40

In Focus

How many dots are there?

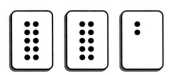

Let us count in twos.

Can we count in fives?

Let's Learn

1

  21
2 0 **1**

20 **1**

  26
20 **6**

  22
20 **2**

  27
20 **7**

  23
20 **3**

  28
20 **8**

  24
20 **4**

  29
20 **9**

  25
20 **5**

 30
20 **10**

2 How many 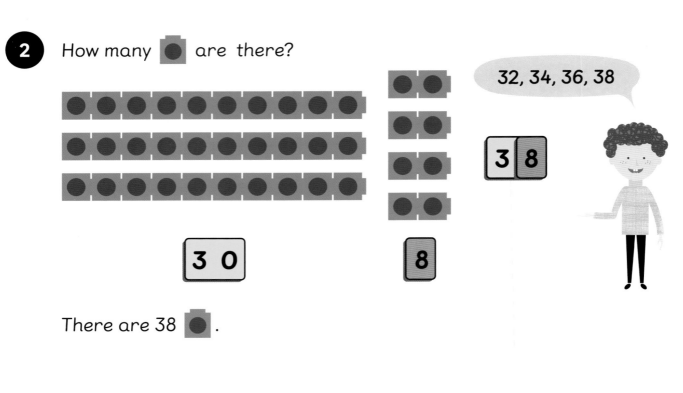 are there?

32, 34, 36, 38

3 8

3 0

8

There are 38 ●.

3 How many ▢ are there?

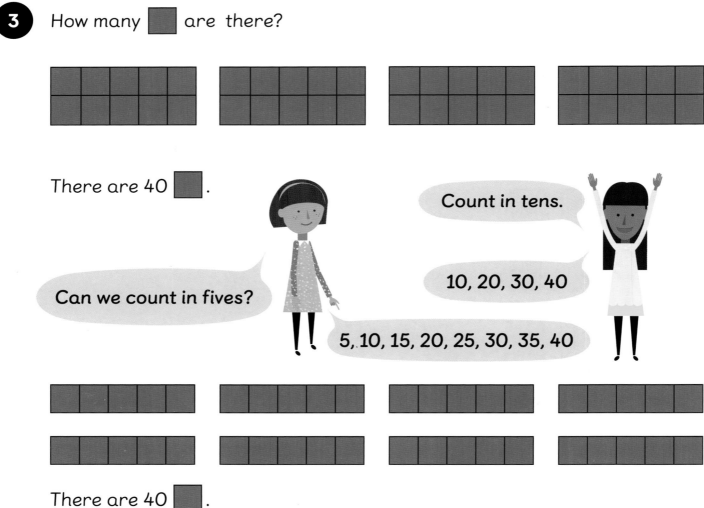

There are 40 ▢.

Can we count in fives?

Count in tens.

10, 20, 30, 40

5, 10, 15, 20, 25, 30, 35, 40

There are 40 ▢.

Guided Practice

1 How many 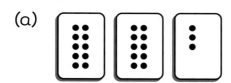 are there?

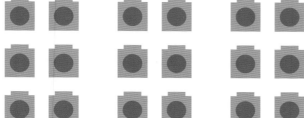

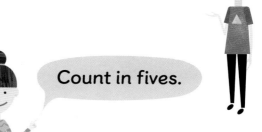

Count in tens.

Count in fives.

Count in twos.

There are [ ]  .

2 How many dots are there?

(a)

There are [ ] dots.

(b)

There are [ ] dots.

(c)

There are [ ] dots.

Complete Worksheet **2** – Page **5 - 6**

Counting in Tens and Ones

In Focus

Count the chocolates.
How many tens and how many ones are there?

There are 32 chocolates.

What does the digit 3 in 32 stand for?
What does the digit 2 in 32 stand for?

3 and 2 are digits.

Let's Learn

We can use to show 32 in tens and ones.

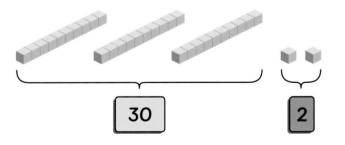

30

2

3 2

32 = 3 tens and 2 ones

30 is the same as 3 tens.
2 is the same as 2 ones.

tens	ones
3	2

This is a **place-value chart**.

Work in pairs.

① Use to show each number in tens and ones.

2 1   2 4   3 0   3 5   3 6

② Write the numbers on a place-value chart.

Guided Practice

Count in tens and ones.

 1

25 =  tens and ⬛ ones

tens	ones

2

34 = ⬛ tens and ⬛ ones

tens	ones

Complete Worksheet 3 – Page 7 - 10 ▶

Comparing Numbers

In Focus

class A

class B

Which class has more pupils?
What can we do to find out?

Let's Learn

1 Which class has more pupils, class A or class B?

Count the number of pupils in each class.
Use to show each number.

class A

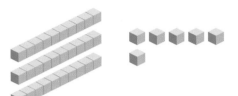

tens	ones
3	6

3 tens and 6 ones = **3 6**

class B

tens	ones
2	7

2 tens and 7 ones = **2 7**

Compare the number of tens.

3 tens is more than 2 tens.

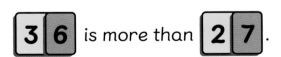
3 6 is more than **2 7**.

2 tens is less than 3 tens.

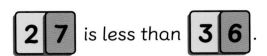
2 7 is less than **3 6**.

Class A has more pupils.
Class B has fewer pupils.

2 Compare the three numbers.

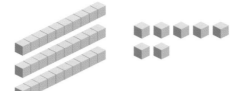

tens	ones
3	7

3 tens and 7 ones = **3** **7**

tens	ones
2	2

2 tens and 2 ones = **2** **2**

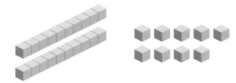

tens	ones
2	9

2 tens and 9 ones = **2** **9**

How can we compare 37 and 22? How about 22 and 29?

3 tens is more than 2 tens.

3 **7** is more than **2** **2**.

3 **7** is more than **2** **9**.

3 **7** is the greatest.

2 ones is less than 9 ones.

2 **2** is less than **2** **9**.

2 **2** is the smallest.

Both 22 and 29 have 2 tens. What should we compare next?

Arrange the numbers in order.

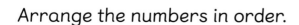

22,	29,	37
smallest ⟶ greatest		

37,	29,	22
greatest ⟶ smallest		

Work in pairs.

What you need:

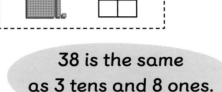

① Pick a number that is more than 20 but less than 40.
Use  to show the number.

② Ask your partner to show you a number that is more than this.

③ Together, choose a third number that is less than this.

④ Write the numbers on [tens|ones].
Arrange the three numbers in order.

38 is the same as 3 tens and 8 ones.

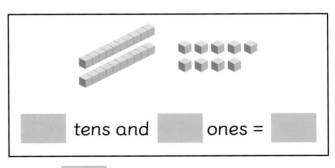

Guided Practice

1 Count and compare.

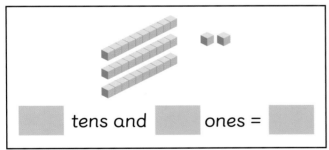

[ ] tens and [ ] ones = [ ]

[ ] tens and [ ] ones = [ ]

[ ] is more than [ ] .

2 Compare 34, 29 and 38.

(a) The greatest number is [ ] .

(b) Arrange the numbers in order. Start with the smallest.

[ ] , [ ] , [ ]

Complete Worksheet 4 – Page **11 – 14**

Finding How Much More

In Focus

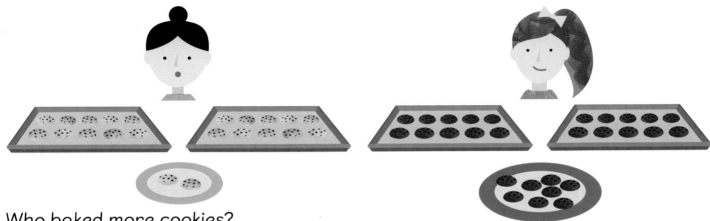

Who baked more cookies?
How many more?

Let's Learn

1

baked 6 more cookies than .

2

| 22 |

28 is more than 22.
28 is 6 more than 22.

| 28 |

22   6

2

What is 1 more than 22?

What is 1 less than 22?

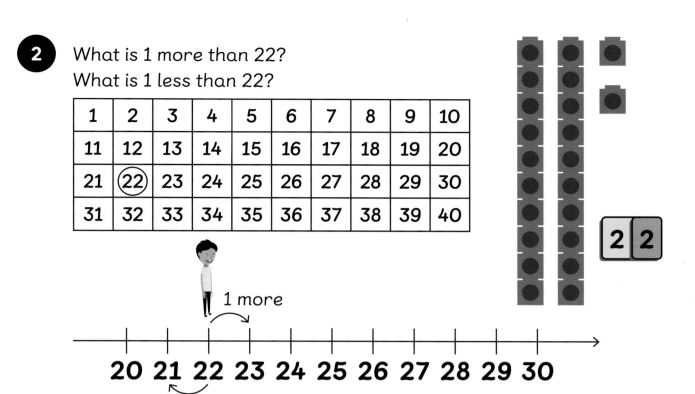

1	2	3	4	5	6	7	8	9	10
11	12	13	14	15	16	17	18	19	20
21	(22)	23	24	25	26	27	28	29	30
31	32	33	34	35	36	37	38	39	40

1 more

20 21 22 23 24 25 26 27 28 29 30

1 less

23 is 1 more than 22.

21 is 1 less than 22.

What is 6 more than 22?

Guided Practice

20 21 22 23 24 25 26 27 28 29 30 31 32 33 34

1 What is 1 more than 32?

What is 1 less than 32?

2 _____ is 1 more than 30.

_____ is 1 less than 30.

1	2	3	4	5	6	7	8	9	10
11	12	13	14	15	16	17	18	19	20
21	22	23	24	25	26	27	28	29	30
31	32	33	34	35	36	37	38	39	40

3 What is 4 less than 31?

What is 4 more than 31?

Complete Worksheet **5** – Page **15 - 16**

Making Number Patterns

1	2	3	4	5	6	7	8	9	10
11	12	13	14	15	16	17	18	19	20
21	22	23	24		26	27		29	30
31	32		34	35	36		38	39	40

What are the missing numbers in the number chart?

Let's Learn

Read aloud the numbers from 1 to 40 and from 40 to 1.

1 What is 1 more than 24?

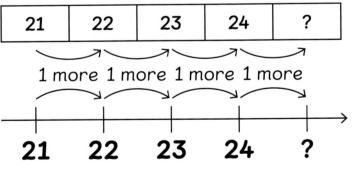

Each number is 1 more than the number before it. What is 1 more than 24?

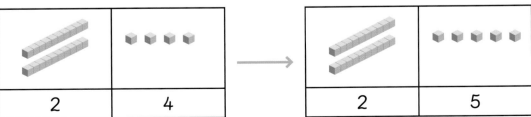

1 more than 24 is 25.
The number pattern is 21, 22, 23, 24, 25.

2 What comes next in the pattern?

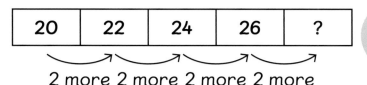

2 more 2 more 2 more 2 more

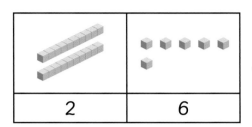 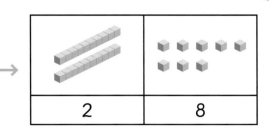

Each number is 2 more than the number before it. What is 2 more than 26?

2 more than 26 is .

The number pattern is 20, 22, 24, 26, ___.

3 What comes next in the pattern?

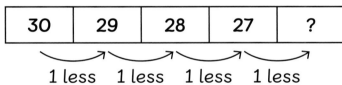

1 less 1 less 1 less 1 less

Each number is 1 less than the number before it. What is 1 less than 27?

1 less than 27 is .

The number pattern is 30, 29, 28, 27, ___.

4 What comes next in the pattern?

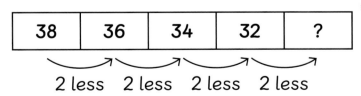

2 less 2 less 2 less 2 less

Each number is 2 less than the number before it. What is 2 less than 32?

2 less than 32 is .

The number pattern is 38, 36, 34, 32, ___.

Work in pairs.

What you need:

21	22	23	24	25	26	27	28	29	30
31	32	33	34	35	36	37	38	39	40

① Put a on the number 21.
Move the  forward 1 number
at a time to find the next number.
Then complete the pattern.

21, 22, 23, 24, ⬜ , ⬜ , ⬜

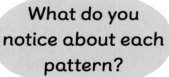

1 more than 21 is 22.

② Use 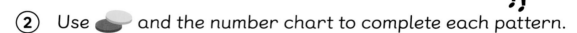 and the number chart to complete each pattern.

(a) 34, 35, 36, 37, ⬜ , ⬜ , ⬜

(b) 28, 27, 26, 25, ⬜ , ⬜ , ⬜

(c) 24, 26, 28, 30, ⬜ , ⬜ , ⬜

(d) 37, 35, 33, 31, ⬜ , ⬜ , ⬜

What do you notice about each pattern?

Can you use a number line to complete the patterns?

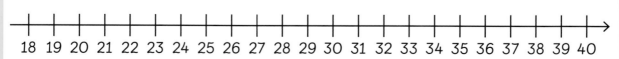

18 19 20 21 22 23 24 25 26 27 28 29 30 31 32 33 34 35 36 37 38 39 40

Guided Practice

1 Find the missing numbers.

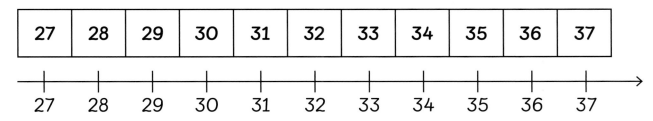

| 27 | 28 | 29 | 30 | 31 | 32 | 33 | 34 | 35 | 36 | 37 |

27 28 29 30 31 32 33 34 35 36 37

(a) ☐ is 1 more than 29.

(b) ☐ is 1 less than 37.

(c) ☐ is 2 more than 31.

(d) ☐ is 2 less than 35.

2 Complete the number patterns.

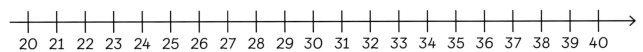

20 21 22 23 24 25 26 27 28 29 30 31 32 33 34 35 36 37 38 39 40

(a) 33, 32, 31, 30, 29, ☐ , ☐ , 26

(b) 26, 28, 30, ☐ , 34, ☐ , 38, ☐

Complete Worksheet 6 – Page 17

Mind Workout

Use the digits to make three 2-digit numbers that are more than 20.

1   **3**   **2**

Write the numbers and arrange them in order.
Start with the smallest.

Make two different number patterns with the numbers given.
Each pattern should have four numbers.
Use each number only once.

I know how to...

Self Check

☐ count in twos, fives and tens.

☐ count within 40.

☐ read and write numbers from 21 to 40.

☐ use a place-value chart to show numbers in tens and ones.

☐ compare and arrange numbers within 40.

☐ find how much more.

☐ complete number patterns.

How many flowers are there in total?

Chapter 11
Addition and Subtraction
Word Problems

Solving Word Problems

There are
8 flowers in the vase.
I am holding
2 flowers.

Should we add or subtract to find the total number of flowers?

Let's Learn

1 There are 8 flowers in the vase.
There are 2 flowers in Hannah's hand.
How many flowers are there in total?

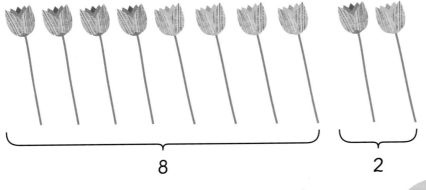

8

2

8   2

10

Why do we add?

$8 + 2 = 10$

There are 10 flowers in total.

2

 3 of the flowers are mine.

 The rest are mine.

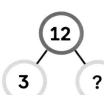

12

3   ?

$12 - 3 = $

 flowers are mine.

Guided Practice

Holly has 7 foreign coins. She also has 9 local coins.

(a) How many coins does Holly have?

 I try to use drawings.

 I try to calculate.

(b) Of the 7 foreign coins, 3 are from Asia and the rest are from South America.

How many coins are from South America?

Complete Worksheet 1 – Page 23 – 24 ▶

Solving Word Problems

In Focus

How many more cubes do they need to make a stack of 10 cubes?

Let's Learn

1

There are 6 cubes now.

How many more to make 10?

$6 + \boxed{} = 10$

2

$6 + 1 = \boxed{}$

$6 + 2 = \boxed{}$

$6 + 3 = \boxed{}$

$6 + \boxed{} = 10$

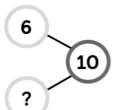

1   How many cubes need to be taken away so that the stack has 4 cubes?

$6 -$ ⬜ $= 4$

2 $9 - 2 =$ ⬜

$9 - 3 =$ ⬜

$9 -$ ⬜ $= 2$

9

○   2

3 $10 +$ ⬜ $= 12$

$10 -$ ⬜ $= 2$

Complete Worksheet **2** – Page **25 - 26**

Solving Word Problems

In Focus

Sam bakes 20 cookies.
What if he gives some away?

Let's Learn

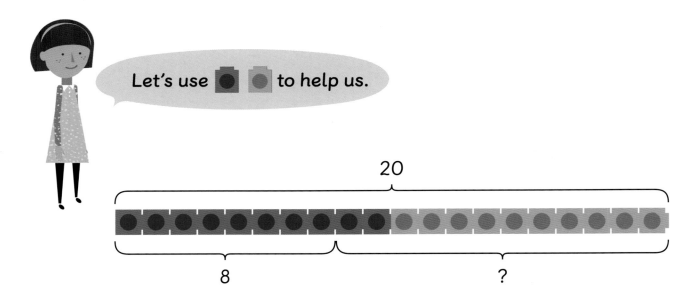

Let's use ● ● to help us.

What if Sam gives away 8 cookies?

20 − 8 = [ ]

Then, Sam would have [ ] cookies left.

1

$$14 - 2 = \boxed{}$$

(10)   (4)

$$14 - 8 = \boxed{}$$

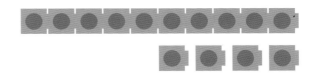
(4)   (10)

2   Ruby has 14 coins.

(a)   What if she gives away 6 coins?

Write an equation.

$$\boxed{} \; \bigcirc \; \boxed{} \; = \; \boxed{}$$

Then, Ruby would have $\boxed{}$ coins.

(b)   Instead, what if she receives another 6 coins?

Write an equation.

$$\boxed{} \; \bigcirc \; \boxed{} \; = \; \boxed{}$$

Then, Ruby would have $\boxed{}$ coins.

Complete Worksheet **3** – Page **27 – 28**

Solving Word Problems

In Focus

Emma has 13 stamps.
Ravi has 3 more stamps than Emma has.

Let's Learn

Show 3 more using ◉.

1 How many stamps does Ravi have?

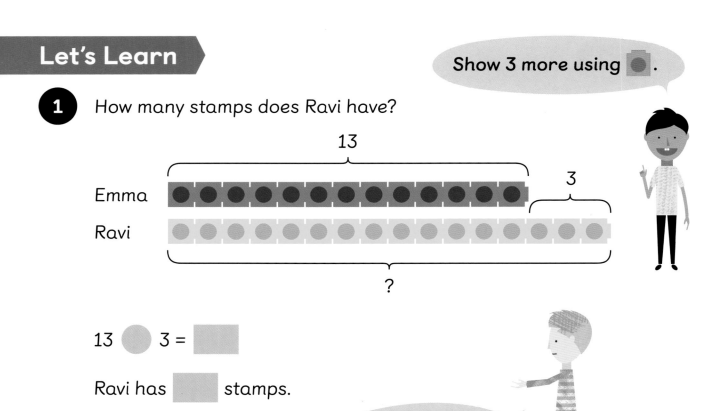

13 ◯ 3 = ▢

Ravi has ▢ stamps.

Should we add or subtract? Why?

2 Hannah has 18 stickers.
Ruby has 7 stickers.
Who has fewer stickers? How many fewer?

Who has fewer stickers, Hannah or Ruby?

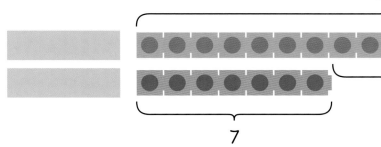

18

7

?

Should we add or subtract? Why?

[ ] ⬤ [ ] = [ ]

Ruby has [ ] fewer stickers than Hannah.

Guided Practice

1 Elliott buys 15 sweets.
Ruby buys 2 more sweets than Elliott buys.
How many sweets does Ruby buy?

2 Emma has 13 goldfish.
She has 6 fewer goldfish than clownfish.
How many clownfish does Emma have?

Complete Worksheet **4** – Page **29 – 30**

Solving Word Problems

In Focus

Holly   Elliott

What is the difference between the number of Elliott's tennis balls and the number of Holly's tennis balls?

Let's Learn

Holly

Elliott

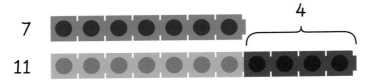

7

11

4

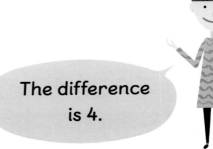

The difference is 4.

$11 - 7 = 4$

The difference between 11 and 7 is 4.

Guided Practice

1 Find the difference between 10 and 8.

10　●●●●●●●●●●

8　●●●●●●●●

2 Find the difference between 12 and 9.

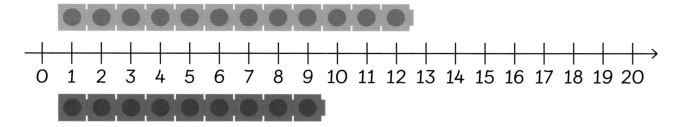

3 Find the difference between

(a)　19 and 7

(b)　20 and 14

Complete Worksheet 5 – Page 31 – 32

Solving Word Problems

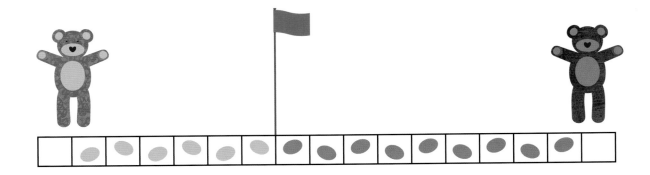

In Focus

How far are 🐻 and 🐻 apart?
What is the distance between them?

Let's Learn

 is 6 ⬭ from ⚑.

🐻 is 9 ⬭ from ⚑.

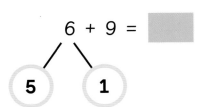

$$6 + 9 = \boxed{}$$

5   1

The distance between 🐻 and 🐻 is ▨ ⬭.

Guided Practice

1

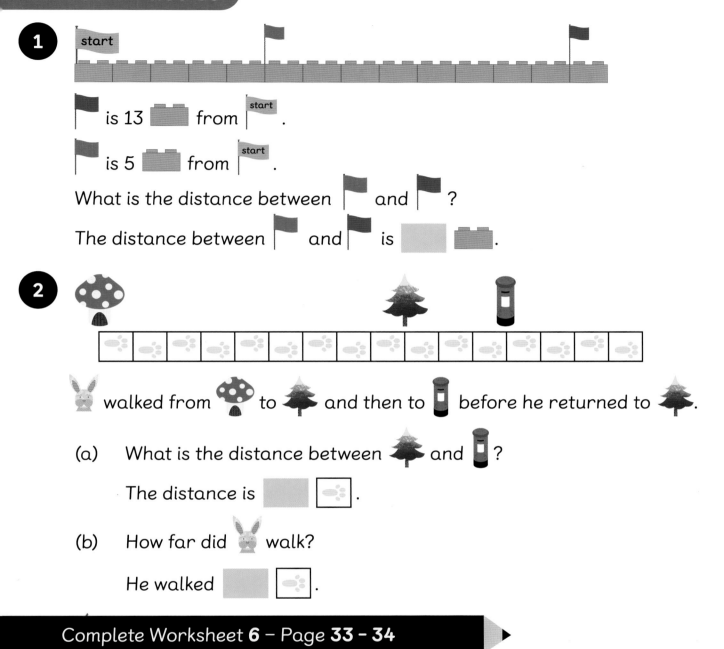

is 13 ⬚ from start.

is 5 ⬚ from start.

What is the distance between 🚩 and 🚩?

The distance between 🚩 and 🚩 is ⬚ ⬚.

2

🐰 walked from 🍄 to 🌲 and then to 📮 before he returned to 🌲.

(a) What is the distance between 🌲 and 📮?

The distance is ⬚ ⬚.

(b) How far did 🐰 walk?

He walked ⬚ ⬚.

Complete Worksheet 6 – Page 33 – 34

Mind Workout

I have 4 more books than Ravi has.
How many books must I give Ravi so that we have the same number of books?

Look at the numbers.

| 11 | 7 |

Use the numbers to make your own word problem.
Show how you solve the word problem.
Draw objects to help you add or subtract.

Sam's Journal

At first, there were 11 snails on a grass patch.
Then, 7 snails crawled away.
How many snails remained on the grass patch?

11 – 7 = 4

4 snails remained on the grass patch.

I know how to...

☐ solve word problems involving addition or subtraction.

Self Check

fruit drinks 5 pack · fruit drinks 5 pack · fruit drinks 5 pack · fruit drinks 5 pack

twin pack · twin pack · twin pack

Which things are in equal groups?

Chapter 12
Multiplication

Making Equal Groups

In Focus

Who made equal groups?

Let's Learn

1

4   4   4

Each plate has 4 .
These are equal groups.

3   5   5

These are not equal groups.

2 Are these equal groups?

There are 2 groups.

Each group has 3 🧁.

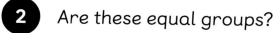

Work in pairs.

What you need:

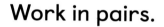

① Make equal groups.
Use fewer than 10 ■.

② Take turns to describe the equal groups.

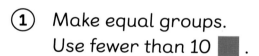

There are ⬜ groups.

Each group has ⬜ tiles.

③ Can you tell your partner the total number of tiles?

1 Which of these show equal groups?

(a)

(b)

(c)

2 (a)

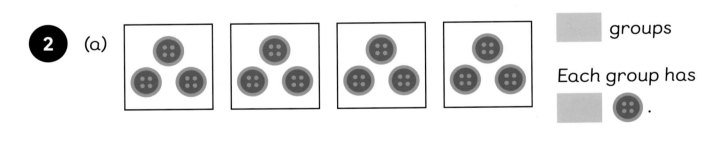

[ ] groups

Each group has

[ ] 🔘 .

(b)

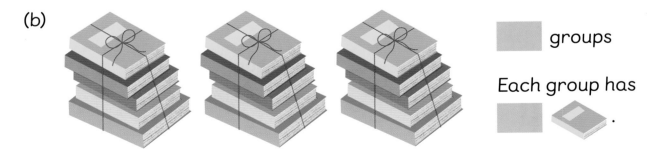

[ ] groups

Each group has

[ ] 📖 .

Complete Worksheet **1** – Page **37 - 38**

Adding Equal Groups

In Focus

 are in equal groups.

How many  are there altogether?

How can you tell?

That means every tray has the same number of .

Let's Learn

1

There are 4 trays.

4 trays of 5 = 20
4 groups of 5 = 20
4 fives = 20

There are 20 altogether.

Each tray has 5 .

5, 10, 15, 20

2

 Each pack has 2 .

There are 3 packs.

3 packs of 2   = 6
3 groups of 2 = 6
3 twos   = 6

2, 4, 6

There are 6 .

3

There are 5 bunches.

Each bunch has 3 .

5 bunches of 3   = ☐

5 groups of ☐   = ☐

☐   threes   = ☐

3, ☐ , ☐ , ☐ , ☐ .

There are ☐ altogether.

Work in pairs.

What you need:

① Take 5 plates.
   Put 2 🔵 on each plate.

② Tell your partner how many 🔵 there are altogether.

③ Take 3 plates.
   Put 6 🔵 on each plate.

④ Tell your partner how many 🔵 there are altogether.

There are 5 groups of 2.

Guided Practice

1 There are ⬜ groups.

Each group has ⬜ apples.

⬜ fours = ⬜

There are ⬜ apples.

2 ⬜ groups of 2 = ⬜

⬜ twos = ⬜

There are ⬜ ribbons altogether.

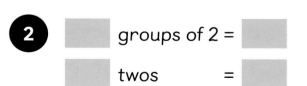 Complete Worksheet **2** · Page **39 – 41**

Making Equal Rows

In Focus

How many  are on the tray?

Let's Learn

1

3 cookies in 1 row

6 cookies in 2 rows

12 cookies in 4 rows

[ ] cookies in 6 rows

6 rows of threes

6 threes

2

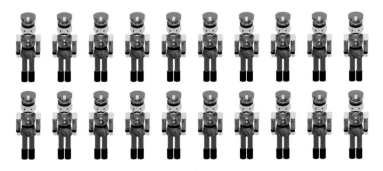

There are 10 toy soldiers in one row.

2 tens = 20

There are 20 toy soldiers altogether.

10, 20

Work in pairs.

What you need:

1. Make equal rows of .

2. Take turns to talk about the rows of 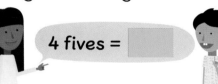.

   4 rows

   5 in one row.

3. Work together to figure out the total number of .

   4 fives =

Guided Practice

1

_____ rows

2 🍋 in one row

_____ twos = _____

There are _____ 🍋 altogether.

2

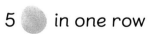

_____ rows

5 in one row

_____ fives = _____

There are _____ altogether.

Complete Worksheet 3 · Page 42 – 43

Making Doubles

In Focus

What happens when we double ?

Let's Learn

1

Double 2 = 4

2 twos

2

Double 5 = 10

2 fives

3

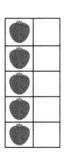
What happens when the beanstalk doubles its height?

Work in pairs.

What you need:

(1) Roll the dice.
Show your partner the correct number of .

(2) Can your partner show you double that number?

(3) Take turns to repeat (1) and (2).

2 threes equal 6.

Guided Practice

1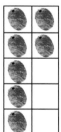

Double 7 = ⬜ sevens

= ⬜

2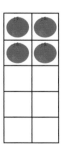

Double 4 = ⬜ fours

= ⬜

3 What is double 8?

Complete Worksheet **4** · Page **44**

Solving Word Problems

In Focus

How many chocolates are there in one box?
How many chocolates are there altogether?

Let's Learn

 1

4 trays of 2 chocolates = 8 chocolates
4 twos = 8

 We say 4 groups of 2 equal 8.

 Let's count 2, 4, 6, 8.

2

2 trays of 8 chocolates = 16 chocolates
2 eights = 16

 We say 2 groups of 8 equal 16.

 Let's add 8 + 8 =

Guided Practice

1 There are 6 sandwiches in each box.
How many sandwiches are there in
these 3 boxes?

2 Holly makes 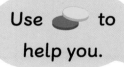 using 3 beads.
How many beads does she need to make 5 of these?

3 (a) 4 groups of 2 = ▢

(b) 4 groups of 5 = ▢

(c) 4 groups of 10 = ▢

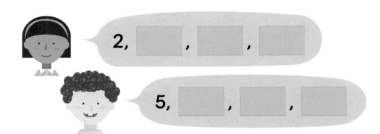

2, ▢ , ▢ , ▢

5, ▢ , ▢ , ▢

4 (a) 5 twos = ▢

(b) 2 nines = ▢

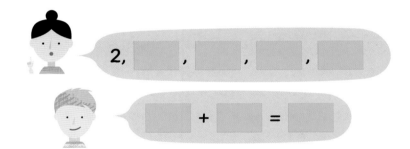

2, ▢ , ▢ , ▢ , ▢

▢ + ▢ = ▢

Complete Worksheet 5 · Page 45 – 47

Mind Workout

Use 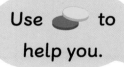 to help you.

Holly wants to buy 8 cupcakes for a party.

She wants to have an equal number of cupcakes in each box.
How many ways can Holly buy the cupcakes?

Look at the picture.

Make three stories about equal groups.
Use these words to help you.

car	train carriage	teacup

I know how to...

☐ make equal groups.

☐ add equal groups to find the total number of objects.

☐ solve word problems about multiplication.

Self Check

How can the girls pack the objects into equal groups?

Chapter 13
Division

Grouping Equally

In Focus

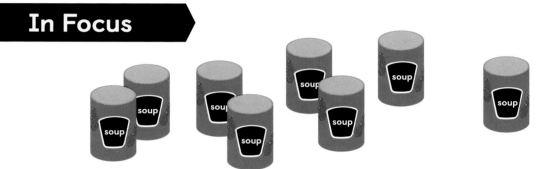

Emma puts 2 cans of tomato soup into a box.
How many boxes does she need for all the cans?

Let's Learn

1 There are 8 cans.

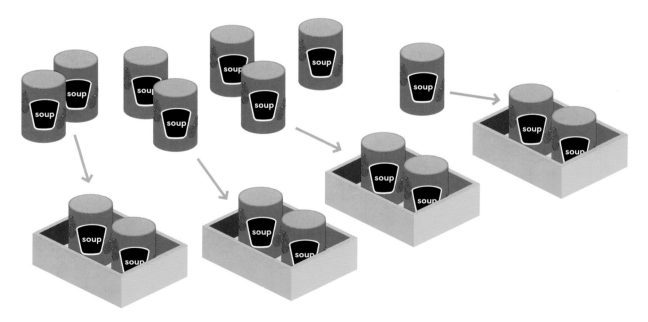

There are 4 boxes of 2 cans.

2 There are 12 flowers.
Lulu uses 3 flowers in each bouquet.
How many bouquets does she get?

She gets 4 bouquets.

3 There are 4 books.
Hannah puts 2 books in each pile.
How many piles of books does she get?

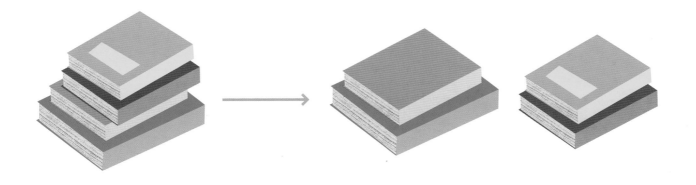

She gets [ ] piles of books.

Work in pairs.

What you need:

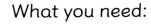

① Count out 24 .

② Put 3 ● on each ◯.

How many plates do we need?

How many different ways can you make equal groups with 24 ●?

③ Make equal groups of different numbers.

Guided Practice

Ravi has 18 pencils.
He puts 6 pencils in each box.
How many boxes does Ravi need?

Ravi needs [ ] boxes.

Complete Worksheet 1 – Page 53 - 56

Sharing Equally

In Focus

There are 6 cookies.
Each child takes the same number of cookies.
How many cookies does each child get?

Let's Learn

1 Each child takes one cookie.

Each child takes one more cookie.

No cookies are left.

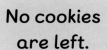

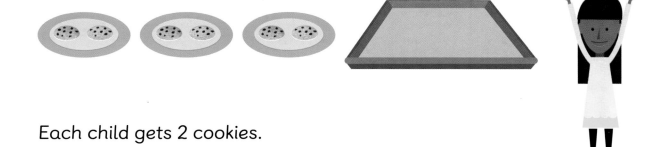

Each child gets 2 cookies.

2 There are 12 toy cars.
Put the toy cars equally into 4 boxes.
How many toy cars are there in each box?

 Circle to make 4 groups.

There are 3 toy cars in each box.

Activity Time

Work in pairs.

What you need:

① Count out 20 .

② Put the equally onto 5 plates.

How many are there on each plate?

Can you put 18 in 5 equal groups? Why or why not?

③ Repeat ① and ② with different numbers of cubes and paper plates.

1 Put 12 cherries equally on 3 slices of cake.
How many cherries are there on each slice of cake?

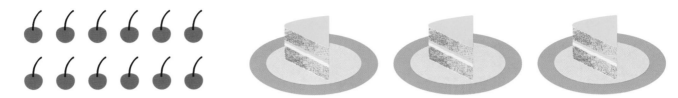

There are ⬜ cherries on each slice of cake.

2 5 children share 10 sweets equally.
How many sweets does each child get?

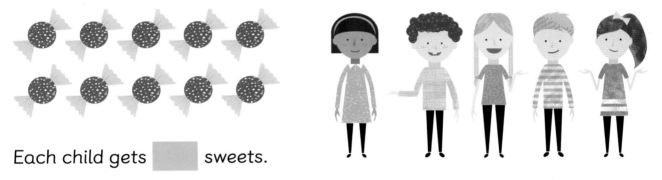

Each child gets ⬜ sweets.

Complete Worksheet **2** – Page **57 - 62**

Mind Workout

Move some balls so that there is the same number of balls in each box.

There will be ⬜ balls in each box.

You can try this using ⬤ and ⭕ .

Holly is making birthday cards for 3 friends.
She wants to put the same number of things on each card.

She has 3   9   12 🌸 15 ⭐

Draw the 3 birthday cards.

I know how to...

☐ group things equally.

☐ share things equally.

Self Check

How can the piece of paper be shared equally?

Chapter 14
Fractions

Making Halves

In Focus

Holly and Charles share
a piece of art paper equally.
In what ways can they do this?

Let's Learn

1

 Are there other ways to do this?

 gets This is half.

 gets This is also half.

2 halves make the whole piece of art paper.

Work in pairs.

① Name the shapes.

② Cut each shape into 2 halves.

③ Paste them in your journal.

What you need:

half   half

Two halves make one whole.

Guided Practice

1 Which of these show halves?

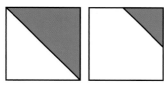  

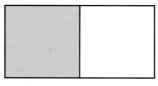 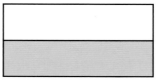

Each shape shows one whole.

2 Shade to show half of the rectangle.

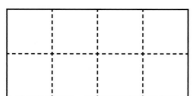

Complete Worksheet 1 – Page 67 – 68 ▶

Making Quarters

In Focus

How can the cake be cut into four equal pieces?

That means each person gets the same amount of cake.

Let's Learn

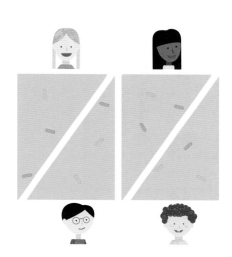

Are these equal?

Are there other ways?

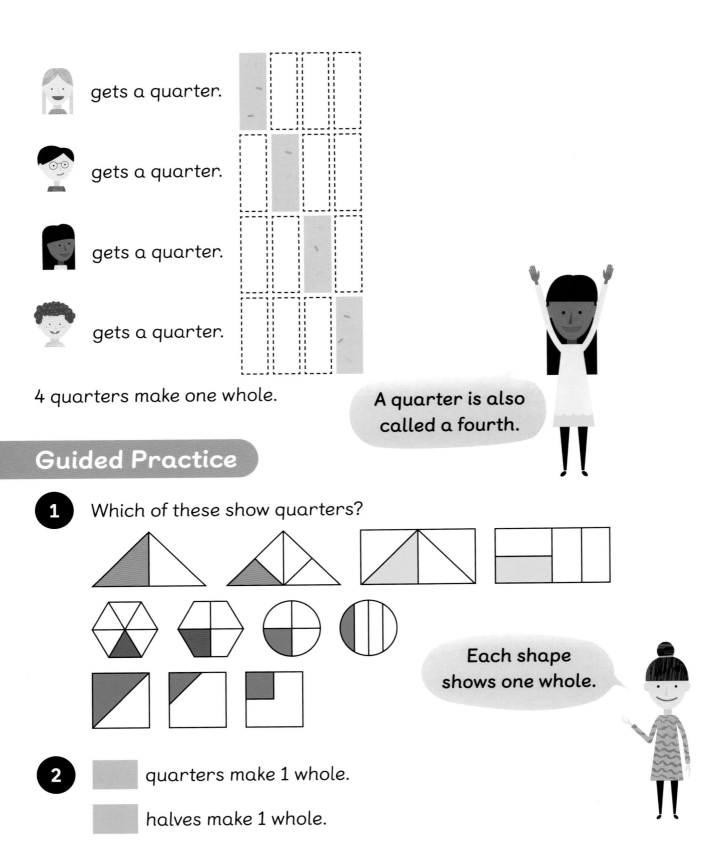

gets a quarter.

gets a quarter.

gets a quarter.

gets a quarter.

4 quarters make one whole.

A quarter is also called a fourth.

Guided Practice

1 Which of these show quarters?

Each shape shows one whole.

2 ▢ quarters make 1 whole.

▢ halves make 1 whole.

▢ quarters make 1 half.

Complete Worksheet **2** – Page **69 – 70**

Sharing and Grouping

In Focus

How do we group the cupcakes equally?

Let's Learn

1

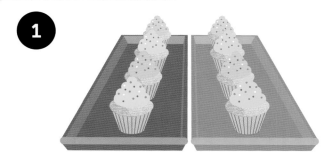

Half of the box of cupcakes

= 4 cupcakes

A quarter of the box of cupcakes

= 2 cupcakes

2

 and are to share the doughnuts.

 gets half of the box.   gets 4 .

 3

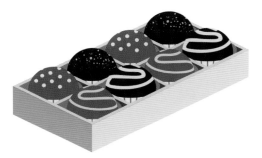

   share the box of chocolates.

 gets a quarter of the box of chocolates.

 gets 2 🧁.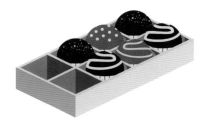

Work in pairs.

What you need:

Is this possible?

① Show your partner some counters.
Use fewer than 20.

② Try to share the counters so each of you gets half of them.

Guided Practice

half	

quarter			

Use 🔵 to help you.

1 gets a quarter of 12 coins.

How many coins does he get?

2 gets half of 10 books.

How many books does she get?

Complete Worksheet 3 – Page 71 – 73

Mind Workout

Who is correct? Explain.

They don't all look the same.

These are not quarters.

Charles

I disagree. I think these are quarters.

Emma

Maths Journal

Make quarters using a square. Paste them in your journal.

Emma's Journal

Method 1		4 quarters make 1 whole.
Method 2		4 quarters make 1 whole.

Find as many different ways to do this as you can.

Self Check

I know how to...

☐ show half.

☐ show a quarter.

☐ group/share things to get a half or a quarter.

☐ find a half or a quarter of a group of things.

How many crayons
are there altogether?

Chapter 15
Numbers to 100

Counting to 100

In Focus

How many crayons are there?

Group them in tens.

Let's Learn

1

1 ten

10 colours

Count in tens.
10 ones = 1 ten

10

2 tens

10 colours 10 colours

20

3 tens

10 colours 10 colours 10 colours

30

4 tens

10 colours 10 colours 10 colours 10 colours

40

5 tens

10 colours 10 colours 10 colours 10 colours 10 colours

50

6 tens

60

7 tens

70

8 tens

80

9 tens

90

10 tens

100

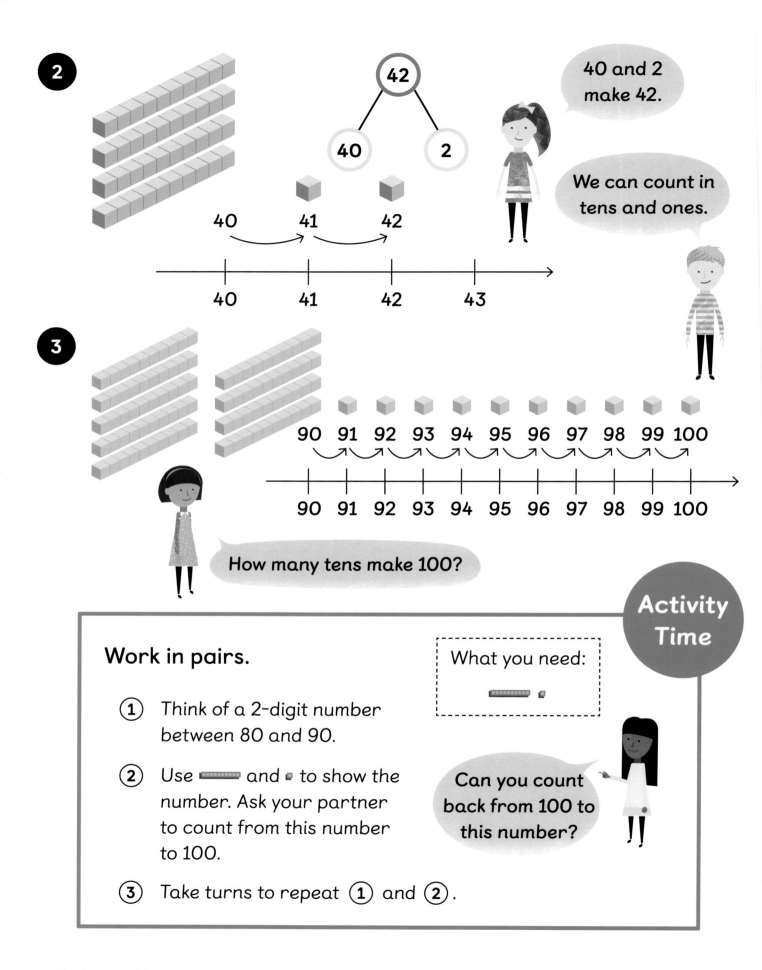

2

42

40   2

40 and 2 make 42.

40   41   42

40   41   42   43

We can count in tens and ones.

3

90 91 92 93 94 95 96 97 98 99 100

90 91 92 93 94 95 96 97 98 99 100

How many tens make 100?

Activity Time

Work in pairs.

What you need:

(1) Think of a 2-digit number between 80 and 90.

(2) Use ▭ and ▪ to show the number. Ask your partner to count from this number to 100.

Can you count back from 100 to this number?

(3) Take turns to repeat (1) and (2).

Count.
Write in numbers.

1

2

3

4

5

Complete Worksheet **1** – Page **77 - 79**

Finding Tens and Ones

In Focus

There are 56 cubes.

What does the digit 5 in 56 stand for?
What does the digit 6 in 56 stand for?

Let's Learn

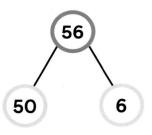

tens	ones
5	6

56 = 5 tens and 6 ones
There are 56 cubes.

The digit **5** in 56 stands for **50**.
The digit **6** in 56 stands for **6**.

Work in pairs.

What you need:

① Think of a 2-digit number between 40 and 100.

② Use ▭▭▭ and ▫ to show the number in tens and ones.

③ Ask your partner to write the number on a place-value chart.

Example

58

tens	ones
5	8

④ Take turns to repeat ① to ③.

Guided Practice

1

66 = ▢ tens and ▢ ones

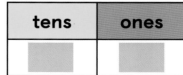

2

▢ = ▢ tens and ▢ ones

Complete Worksheet 2 – Page 80 – 83 ▶

Comparing Numbers

In Focus

Sam   Ruby   Charles

Who has the most coins?
Who has the least number of coins?

Compare the number of coins.

Ruby

Sam

Charles

tens	ones
7	5

75 = 7 tens and 5 ones

tens	ones
6	3

63 = 6 tens and 3 ones

tens	ones
6	9

69 = 6 tens and 9 ones

7 tens is more than 6 tens.
75 is more than 63.
75 is more than 69.

3 ones is less than 9 ones.
63 is less than 69.

Compare the number of tens.

Both 63 and 69 have 6 tens. What should we compare next?

We can arrange the numbers in order.

75,   69,   63

greatest ——→ smallest

63,   69,   75

smallest ——→ greatest

Play in pairs.

What you need:

① Take turns to take two .
Use the digits to make a 2-digit number.

② Compare the numbers.
The player with the greater
2-digit number wins!

**Which is more,
27 or 72?**

Example

7	2

more

2	7

less

Guided Practice

1 Compare the numbers.

tens	ones

tens	ones

☐ = ☐ tens and ☐ ones

☐ = ☐ tens and ☐ ones

☐ is more than ☐ .

2 Arrange the numbers in order.
Start with the smallest.

78,   87,   76

☐ , ☐ , ☐

Complete Worksheet 3 – Page 84 – 89

Making Number Patterns

In Focus

1	2	3	4	5	6	7	8	9	10
11	12	13	14	15	16	17	18	19	20
21	22	23	24	25	26	27	28	29	30
31	32	33	34	35	36	37	38	39	40
41	42	43	44	45	46	47	48	49	50
51	52	53	54	55	56	57	58	59	60
61	62	63	64	65	66	67	68	69	70
71	72	73	74	75	76	77	78	79	80
81	82	83	84	85	86	87	88	89	90
91	92	93	94	95	96	97	98	99	100

This is a one hundred chart.

Look at the numbers in the yellow boxes.
What number patterns do you see?

Let's Learn

1 What is 1 more than 42?

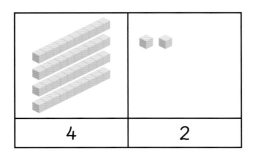

4	2

→ 1 more →

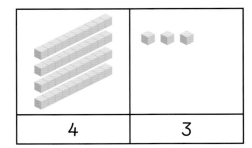

4	3

1 more than 42 is 43.

We can make a number pattern. Each number is 1 more than the number before it.

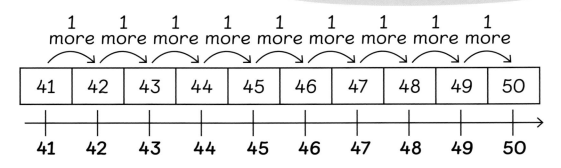

41	42	43	44	45	46	47	48	49	50

2 What is 1 less than 49?

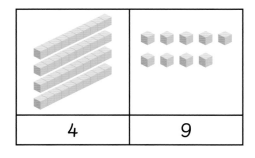

4	9

→ 1 less →

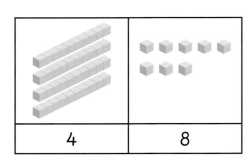

4	8

1 less than 49 is 48.

We can make a number pattern. Each number is ▇ less than the number before it.

49	48	47	46	45	44	43	42	41	40

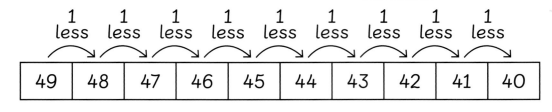

3 Count in twos.

2, 4, 6, 8, 10, 12, ...

84, 86, 88, 90, 92, ...

1	2	3	4	5	6	7	8	9	10
11	12	13	14	15	16	17	18	19	20
21	22	23	24	25	26	27	28	29	30
31	32	33	34	35	36	37	38	39	40
41	42	43	44	45	46	47	48	49	50
51	52	53	54	55	56	57	58	59	60
61	62	63	64	65	66	67	68	69	70
71	72	73	74	75	76	77	78	79	80
81	82	83	84	85	86	87	88	89	90
91	92	93	94	95	96	97	98	99	100

4 Count in fives.

5, 10, 15, 20, 25, ...

55, 60, 65, 70, 75, 80, ...

1	2	3	4	5	6	7	8	9	10
11	12	13	14	15	16	17	18	19	20
21	22	23	24	25	26	27	28	29	30
31	32	33	34	35	36	37	38	39	40
41	42	43	44	45	46	47	48	49	50
51	52	53	54	55	56	57	58	59	60
61	62	63	64	65	66	67	68	69	70
71	72	73	74	75	76	77	78	79	80
81	82	83	84	85	86	87	88	89	90
91	92	93	94	95	96	97	98	99	100

1 Complete the number patterns.

(a)
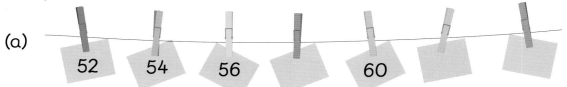
52 54 56   60

(b)
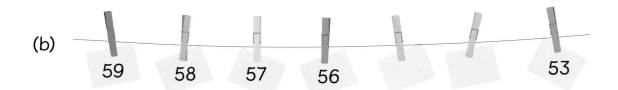
59 58 57 56   53

(c)
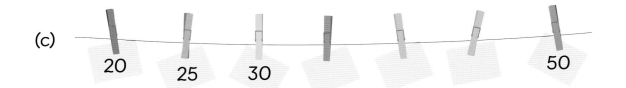
20 25 30   50

2 (a) What number is 1 more than 47?

45 46 47 48 49

(b) What number is 1 more than 59?

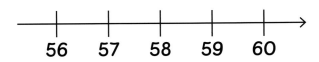
56 57 58 59 60

(c) What number is 1 less than 80?

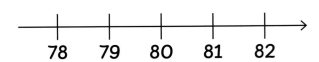
78 79 80 81 82

Complete Worksheet 4 – Page 90 – 91

Look at the digits.

4	8	9

The greatest 2-digit number I can make is ⬜ .

The smallest 2-digit number I can make is ⬜ .

Make two more 2-digit numbers.

Arrange the numbers in order.

⬜ , ⬜ , ⬜ , ⬜

                                         greatest

What is your favourite 2-digit number?
Why?

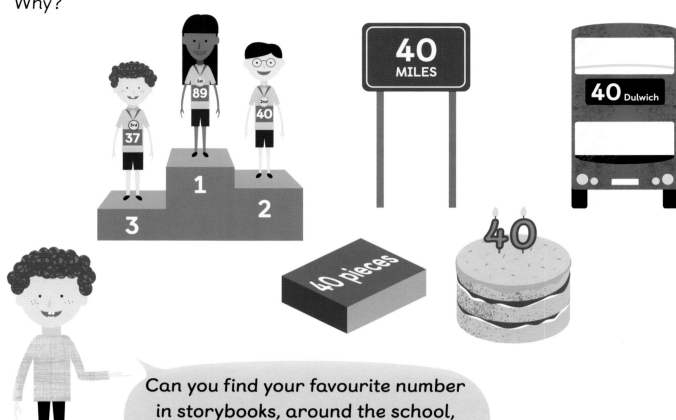

Can you find your favourite number in storybooks, around the school, at home or in your neighbourhood?

Self Check

I know how to...

☐ count to 100.

☐ count in twos, fives and tens to 100.

☐ read and write numbers to 100.

☐ say a number that is 1 more or 1 less than a 2-digit number.

☐ compare and arrange numbers within 100.

Chapter 16
Time

Telling Time to the Hour

In Focus

Look at the clock.
What time does it show?

Let's Learn

1

Can you tell if it is morning, afternoon, evening or night from the clock?

 This is the **minute** hand.

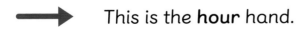 This is the **hour** hand.

The minute hand is pointing to 12.
The hour hand is pointing to 8.
The time is 8 **o'clock**.

2 What time does each clock show?

12 o'clock		2 o'clock	3 o'clock
4 o'clock	5 o'clock		7 o'clock
8 o'clock	9 o'clock	10 o'clock	

Work in pairs.

What you need:

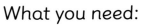

① Move the hands of the .
Ask your partner to read the .

② Talk about the activities you do at that time.

③ Take turns to repeat ① and ②.

I watch television at 8 o'clock at night.

I have music lessons at 8 o'clock in the morning.

What is the time?

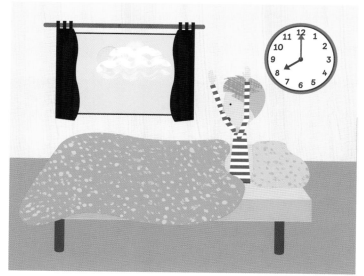

It is 8 o'clock in the morning.

It is [   ] in the morning.

It is [   ] in the afternoon.

It is [   ] in the evening.

Complete Worksheet 1 – Page 101 – 104

Telling Time to the Half Hour

In Focus

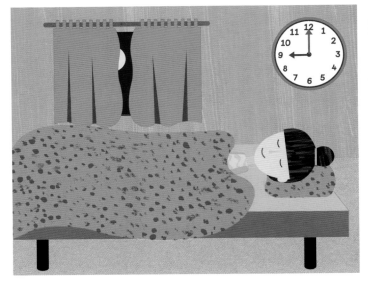

What time do Emma and Ravi go to bed at night?

Let's Learn

The minute hand is pointing to 12. Emma goes to bed at 9 o'clock.

The minute hand is pointing to 6. Ravi goes to bed at **half past** 9.

Where is the hour hand pointing?

The hour hand is between 9 and 10. It has gone past 9.

Using Next, Before and After

In Focus

Ravi wrote down things that he did yesterday evening.

 5 o'clock

I played with my toys.

6 o'clock

I read some stories.

 half past 7

I did my homework.

 8 o'clock

I got ready for bed.

 7 o'clock

I watched TV.

 half past 6

I had a bath.

 half past 8

I went to sleep.

What did he do first?
What did he do last?

1

first

5 o'clock

At 5 o'clock in the evening, he played with his toys.

second

6 o'clock

At 6 o'clock in the evening, he read some stories.

third

half past 6

At half past six in the evening, he had a bath.

fourth

7 o'clock

At 7 o'clock in the evening, he watched TV.

fifth

half past 7

At half past seven in the evening, he did his homework.

sixth

8 o'clock

At 8 o'clock at night, he got ready for bed.

seventh

half past 8

At half past eight at night, he went to sleep.

2

7 o'clock

I watched TV.

What did Ravi do **next**?

half past 7

I did my homework.

 3

half past 6

I had a bath.

What did he do **before** his bath?
What did he do **after** his bath?

6 o'clock

I read some stories before my bath.

7 o'clock

I watched TV after my bath.

This is Holly's timetable for Monday morning.

 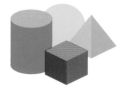 maths

  reading

  break

  P.E.

  spelling

(a)   What did she study at ?

(b)   What did she study at half past nine?

(c)   What did she have before break?

(d)   What did she have after break?

(e)   After P.E, what did she have next?

Complete Worksheet **3** – Page **109**

Estimating Duration of Time

In Focus

maths lesson

music lesson

How long is a second?

Is singing a song likely to take a minute or an hour?

Let's Learn

Clap three times.

That is about one second.

Sing a song.

That is about one minute.

Have a maths lesson.

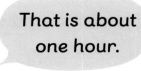
That is about one hour.

Work in groups of 3 to 4.

What you need:

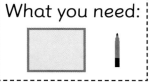

① The teacher will do an activity with you.

② After that, discuss with your friends.

Did it take 5 seconds?

It seemed to take 10 seconds.

How long did that activity take?

③ Write your estimate on ☐ .

Guided Practice

Fill in the blanks with **seconds, minutes, hours, days** or **weeks**.

1 A train ride from one side of London to the other takes about

30 ⬜ .

2 I sleep for about 8 ⬜ each day.

3 I take about 5 ⬜ to walk from one part of the room to another.

Complete Worksheet 4 – Page **110** ▶

Comparing Time

In Focus

Holly

Elliott

Both started folding at the same time. Who was quicker? Who was slower?

Let's Learn

1. Holly and Elliott started making paper aeroplanes at the same time.
   Holly finished making her aeroplane before Elliott did.

   Holly was **quicker** than Elliott in making a paper aeroplane.
   Elliott was **slower** than Holly in making a paper aeroplane.

2

Both Lulu and Sam left their homes at 8 o'clock in the morning.

Lulu arrived in school at half past 8.

Sam arrived in school at 9 o'clock.

Lulu arrived in school **earlier** than Sam did.
Sam arrived in school **later** than Lulu did.

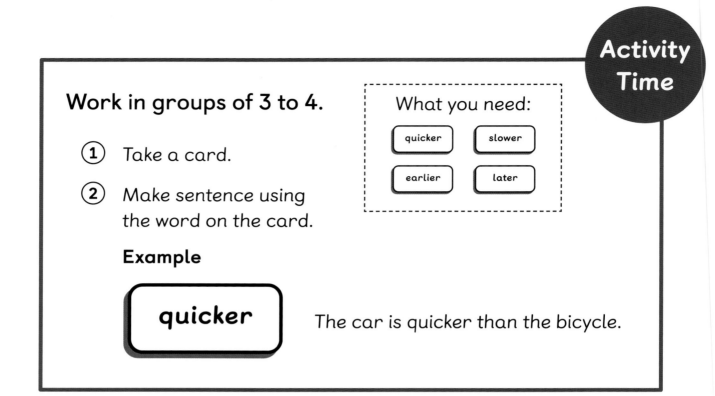

Activity Time

Work in groups of 3 to 4.

What you need:

quicker   slower   earlier   later

① Take a card.

② Make sentence using the word on the card.

Example

quicker   The car is quicker than the bicycle.

Guided Practice

Complete each sentence using **quicker, slower, earlier** or **later.**

(a) The leopard is _____ than the deer it is chasing.

(b) Yesterday, I got home at 4 o'clock. Today, I got home at 3 o'clock.
I got home _____ today.

(c) The tortoise was _____ than the hare but it won the race in the end.

(d) The cartoon started at 7 o'clock which is _____ than its usual time of 6 o'clock.

Complete Worksheet **5** – Page **111**

Using a Calendar

In Focus

October						2014
Mon	**Tues**	**Wed**	**Thurs**	**Fri**	**Sat**	**Sun**
		1	2	3	4	5
6	7	8	9	10	11	12
13	14	15	16	17	18	19
20	21	22	23	24	25	26
27	28	29	30	31		

This is for the year 2014.

Can you name all the days of the week?

Let's Learn

 1 There are 7 days in one week.

The days of the week are **Monday, Tuesday, Wednesday, Thursday, Friday, Saturday** and **Sunday**.

The first day of the week is Monday.
The last day of the week is Sunday.

The days from Monday to Friday are called **weekdays**.
Saturday and Sunday are called **weekends**.

The day after Sunday is Monday.

2

October						2014
Mon	**Tues**	**Wed**	**Thurs**	**Fri**	**Sat**	**Sun**
		1	2	3	4	5
6	7	8	9	10	11	12
13	14	15	16	17	18	19
20	21	22	23	24	25	26
27	28	29	30	31		

October is a month of the year.

There are 3 complete weeks in October.
There are 31 days in October.

The first day of the month falls on a Wednesday.
The last day of the month falls on a Friday.

Calendar 2014

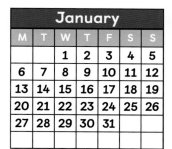

January

M	T	W	T	F	S	S
		1	2	3	4	5
6	7	8	9	10	11	12
13	14	15	16	17	18	19
20	21	22	23	24	25	26
27	28	29	30	31		

February

M	T	W	T	F	S	S
					1	2
3	4	5	6	7	8	9
10	11	12	13	14	15	16
17	18	19	20	21	22	23
24	25	26	27	28		

March

M	T	W	T	F	S	S
					1	2
3	4	5	6	7	8	9
10	11	12	13	14	15	16
17	18	19	20	21	22	23
24	25	26	27	28	29	30
31						

April

M	T	W	T	F	S	S
	1	2	3	4	5	6
7	8	9	10	11	12	13
14	15	16	17	18	19	20
21	22	23	24	25	26	27
28	29	30				

May

M	T	W	T	F	S	S
			1	2	3	4
5	6	7	8	9	10	11
12	13	14	15	16	17	18
19	20	21	22	23	24	25
26	27	28	29	30	31	

June

M	T	W	T	F	S	S
						1
2	3	4	5	6	7	8
9	10	11	12	13	14	15
16	17	18	19	20	21	22
23	24	25	26	27	28	29
30						

July

M	T	W	T	F	S	S
	1	2	3	4	5	6
7	8	9	10	11	12	13
14	15	16	17	18	19	20
21	22	23	24	25	26	27
28	29	30	31			

August

M	T	W	T	F	S	S
				1	2	3
4	5	6	7	8	9	10
11	12	13	14	15	16	17
18	19	20	21	22	23	24
25	26	27	28	29	30	31

September

M	T	W	T	F	S	S
1	2	3	4	5	6	7
8	9	10	11	12	13	14
15	16	17	18	19	20	21
22	23	24	25	26	27	28
29	30					

October

M	T	W	T	F	S	S
		1	2	3	4	5
6	7	8	9	10	11	12
13	14	15	16	17	18	19
20	21	22	23	24	25	26
27	28	29	30	31		

November

M	T	W	T	F	S	S
					1	2
3	4	5	6	7	8	9
10	11	12	13	14	15	16
17	18	19	20	21	22	23
24	25	26	27	28	29	30

December

M	T	W	T	F	S	S
1	2	3	4	5	6	7
8	9	10	11	12	13	14
15	16	17	18	19	20	21
22	23	24	25	26	27	28
29	30	31				

This is a calendar that shows the months of the year.

There are 12 months in one year.

The first month of every year is January.
The last month of every year is December.

Can you name all the months of the year?

Activity Time

Work in pairs.

May	December	April	November
August	March	June	January
October	July	September	February

What you need:

1. Put the cards face down on the table.
2. Mix all the cards.
3. Turn the cards over.
4. Help each other to put the months in the correct order.

Guided Practice

Write the missing words.

1 (a) The last weekday of the week is _____ .

(b) The fourth day of the week is _____ .

(c) Tuesday is the day just before _____ .

2 (a) The seventh month of the year is _____ .

(b) _____ has the least number of days in the year.

(c) The month just after August is _____ .

 Complete Worksheet **6** – Page **112 – 113** ▶

Match.

Ravi   Charles   Holly

            ●   ●

●   ●   ●

Ravi left school after Holly.

Charles left school before Ravi.

Holly left school before Charles.

At what time did each of them leave the school?

Maths Journal

Talk about what you do on Saturday.
Show the time.

 Use a  to show the time.

My Saturday

I wake up at 8 o'clock.	
I eat breakfast at _____.	
I watch television at _____.	
I go outside to play at _____.	

I know how to...

Self Check

☐ tell time to the hour.

☐ tell time to the half hour.

☐ compare different times.

☐ recognise dates on a calendar.

How much money is Emma giving to the cashier?

Chapter 17
Money

Recognising Coins

In Focus

What coins are these?

Let's Learn

 1 pence

 20 pence

 2 pence

 50 pence

 5 pence

 1 pound

 10 pence

 2 pounds

Work in pairs.

What you need:

① The teacher will ask you to guess the coin in his or her hand. You may get hints.

② Make a guess and write it on ☐.

Guided Practice

1 Which of these are 50 pence coins?

2 What coins are these?

Complete Worksheet 1 – Page 119 - 121

Recognising Notes

In Focus

What notes are these?

Let's Learn

 5 pounds

 10 pounds

 20 pounds

 50 pounds

Guided Practice

1 Which of these is a 20-pound note?

2 What notes are these?

3

How many are there?

5-pound notes

10-pound note

20-pound notes

50-pound note

4 Which of these can get you the greatest number of books?

£5 each

Complete Worksheet **2** – Page **122 – 124**

Which notes can pay for the teddy bear?

£15

Maths Journal

A larger coin has a larger value than a smaller coin.

Sam

Is Sam correct?

I know how to...

☐ recognise coins.

☐ recognise notes.

Self Check

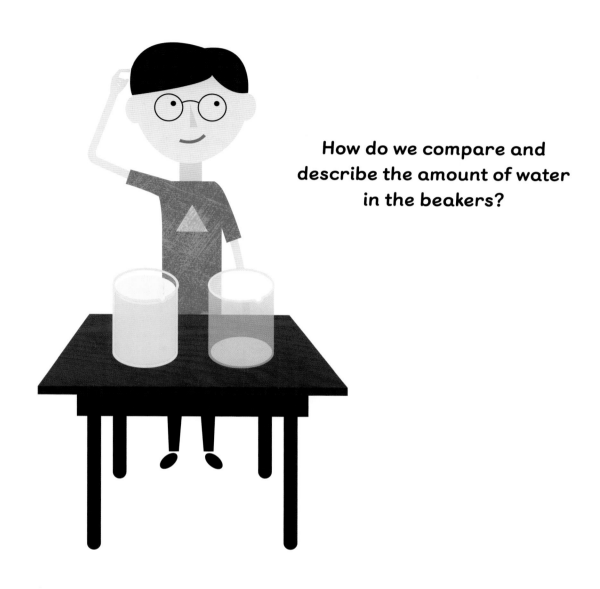

How do we compare and
describe the amount of water
in the beakers?

Chapter 18
Volume and Capacity

Comparing Volume and Capacity

In Focus

How can we compare and describe
the amount of water inside the beakers?

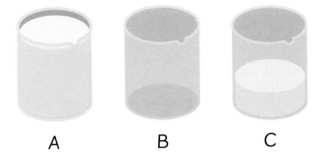

A   B   C

Let's Learn

1

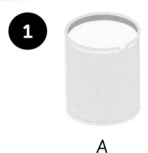

A

Beaker A cannot hold any more water.
Beaker A is **full**.

2

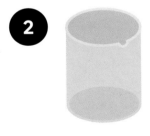

B

Beaker B has no water.
Beaker B is **empty**.

3

A   C

The amount of water in Beaker A is
more than the amount of water in Beaker C.

The amount of water in Beaker C is
less than the amount of water in Beaker A.

Play in groups of 3 to 4.

① Start with an empty ▯.

② Each player takes turns to fill ▯ with either one or two ∕.

Make it full and you lose.

③ The first player to fill the ▯ so that the water overflows loses the game. The player who went before this wins the game.

Guided Practice

Compare using **more than** or **less than**.

(a)

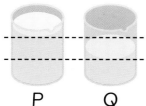

P   Q

The amount of water in Beaker P
is ▭ the amount in Beaker Q.

The amount of water in Beaker Q
is ▭ the amount in Beaker P.

(b)

R   S   T

The amount of water in Beaker S
is ▭ the amount in Beaker R,
and ▭ the amount in Beaker T.

Complete Worksheet 1 – Page 127

Finding Volume and Capacity

In Focus

Which has a greater capacity, the bottle or the mug?

Let's Learn

We use one cup as one unit.

The bottle and mug are filled with water.

Water from the bottle fills 3 cups.
Water from the mug fills 2 cups.

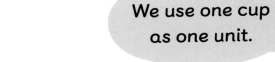
Can we use other containers other than cups?

The capacity of the bottle is 3 units.
The capacity of the mug is 2 units.

The bottle has a greater capacity than the mug.

Work in pairs.

What you need:

(1) Look for containers around you.

(2) Guess the capacity of each container.

(3) Use  to measure the capacity.

Example

Your bottle	I guess the capacity is about ⬜ units.
	The capacity is about ⬜ units.

Guided Practice

Measure.

Each  is 1 unit.

(a)

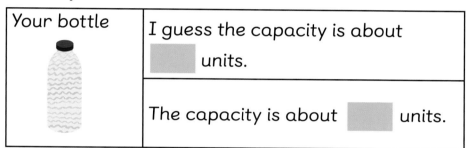

The capacity of the container is about ⬜ units.

(b)

The amount of water in the bowl is about ⬜ units.

Complete Worksheet 2 – Page **128 – 129**

Describing Volume Using Half and a Quarter

In Focus

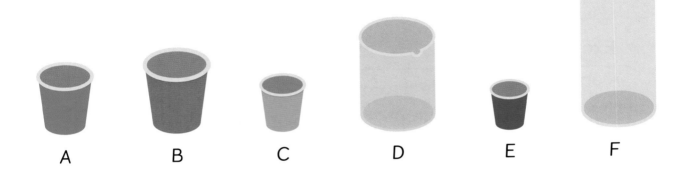

A   B   C   D   E   F

Which container can hold half as much water as [ ] ?

Which container can hold a quarter as much water as [ ] ?

The **capacity** of a container is how much water it can hold.

1 We pour water from the beaker into the empty container.

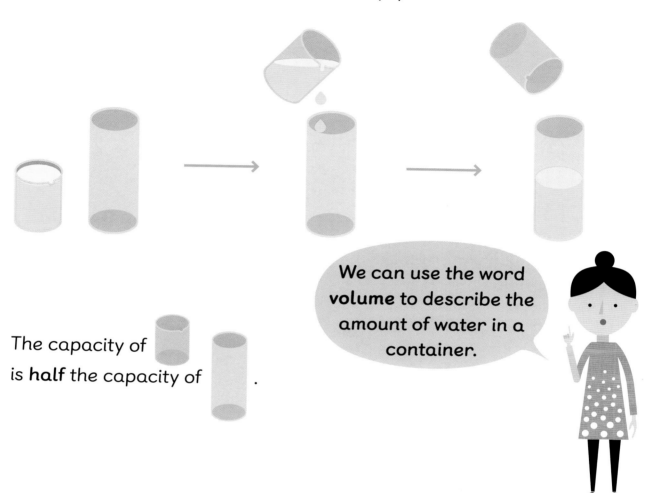

The capacity of is **half** the capacity of .

We can use the word **volume** to describe the amount of water in a container.

2

The container can be filled up with 4 cups of water.
The capacity of one cup is **a quarter** of the capacity of the container.

Work in pairs.

① Guess which containers hold half as much water as a large container.

② Use water to check if your guess is correct.

> How can you tell if a container holds half as much water as the large container?

> Does the cup hold as much water as the large container?

③ Repeat ① and ② to check which containers hold a quarter as much water as the large container.

Fill in the blanks with **2**, **half** or **a quarter**.

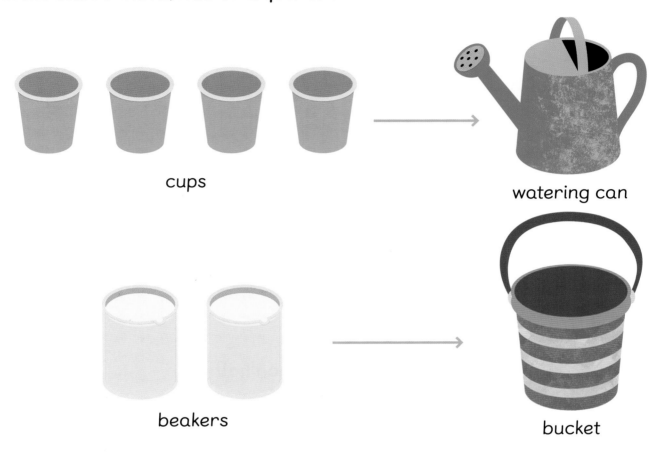

cups

watering can

beakers

bucket

(a) The capacity of one cup is [   ] of the capacity of the watering can.

(b) The volume of water in one beaker is [   ] the volume of water in the bucket.

(c) After the bucket is filled with 1 beaker of water, the bucket is [   ] full.

(d) After the watering can is filled with [   ] cups of water, the watering can is half full.

Complete Worksheet **3** – Page **130 – 131**

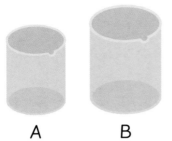

tank   A   B

Pour water from the tank to the beakers back and forth.

The volume of water in the tank is 8 units.
The capacity of beaker A is 3 units.
The capacity of beaker B is 5 units.

Show how the tank and beaker B can have 4 units of water each.

Maths Journal

Describe using **more than half** or **less than half**.

(a)   The capacity of beaker A is _____ the capacity of the tank.

(b)   The capacity of beaker B is _____ the capacity of the tank.

Self Check

I know how to...

☐ compare volume and capacity.

☐ use half and a quarter to describe volume.

☐ find volume and capacity.

Which objects
are heavy and which are light?

Chapter 19
Mass

Comparing Mass

In Focus

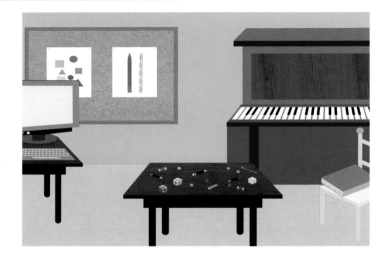

Can you group the objects into heavy and light objects?

Let's Learn

heavy	light
monitor, pin board, chair, piano, table	cube, rubber, keyboard, sweet, marble

The monitor, pin board, chair, piano and table are **heavy** objects.

The cube, rubber, keyboard, sweet and marble are **light** objects.

2

The cube is **heavier than** the rubber.
The rubber is **lighter than** the cube.

The cube is **as heavy as** the marble.

Work in groups.

What you need:

① Choose any two objects from the objects around you.

② Guess the heavier or lighter object.

③ Place each object on one side of the balance scales and write the result.

Example

The paper clip is **heavier** than the sweet.

Guided Practice

1 Group each of the following into **heavy** and **light** objects.

car   feather   apple   paper

football   television   house   whale

2 Compare using **heavier than**, **lighter than** or **as heavy as**.

(a)

The watermelon is [   ]
the bunch of bananas.

(b)

The pen is [   ] the pencil.

(c)

The clock is [   ] the book.

Complete Worksheet 1 – Page 135 – 136

Finding Mass

In Focus

How do we find the mass of the toy car?

Let's Learn

1

The toy car is as heavy as 5 .

The mass of the toy car is about 5 units.

1 ▮ can be used to mean 1 unit.

2

The pair of boots is as heavy as 8 ▮ .

The mass of the pair of boots is about 8 units.

Can we use other objects to measure mass?

Work in pairs.

What you need:

① Look for objects around you.

② Guess the mass of each object.

③ Use ◼ to measure the mass.

Example

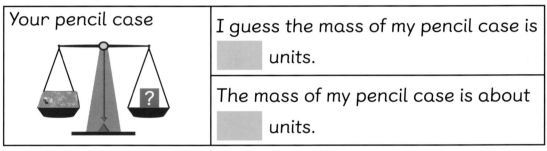

| Your pencil case | I guess the mass of my pencil case is ◻ units. |
| | The mass of my pencil case is about ◻ units. |

Guided Practice

Measure.

1 1 ◼ shows 1 unit.

The mass of the jar is about ◻ units.

2 1 ▲ shows 1 unit.

The mass of the rubber duck is about ◻ units.

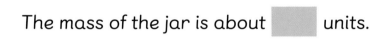

Complete Worksheet **2** – Page **137 – 138** ▶

There are more ● than ■.
The pair of scissors is heavier
than the roll of tape.

Is Lulu correct? Why or why not?

Which is the heavier thing? The pair of scissors or the roll of tape?

beach ball

tennis ball

Which ball is bigger : the beach ball or the tennis ball?

Which ball do you think is heavier : the beach ball or the tennis ball?

Sam thinks that a bigger object is always heavier.

Is it true?

I know how to...

☐ compare mass of objects.

☐ find mass of objects.

Self Check

Are we able to describe
everyone's position?

Chapter 20
pace

Describing Positions

In Focus

How is everyone seated?

Let's Learn

1

Elliott   Sam   Hannah

Elliott, Sam and Hannah are seated on the **top** row.

Ruby   Amira   Emma   Charles

Ruby, Amira, Emma, and Charles are seated in the **middle** row.

Holly   Ravi   Lulu

Holly, Ravi and Lulu are seated on the **bottom** row.

2

Elliott

Amira Emma

Holly

Holly is seated **in front of** Amira, Emma and Elliott.
Amira and Emma are seated in front of Elliott.

Elliott is seated **behind** Amira, Emma and Holly.
Amira and Emma are seated behind Holly.

3

bun ←

tomato ←

meat ←

cheese ←

lettuce ←

bun ←

The buns are at the **top** and **bottom**.

The tomato is **above** the meat, cheese and lettuce.
The meat and cheese are above the lettuce.

The tomato is **on top of** the meat.
The meat is on top of the cheese.

Ravi

Amira

Sam

Emma

Charles

Elliott

Lulu

Holly

Ruby

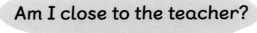

desk

teacher

The children are seated **close** to each other. The children are seated **around** Charles.

The desk is **near** Lulu, Holly and Ruby. The teacher is **close** to the desk.

Ravi, Amira and Sam are seated **far** from the teacher.

Am I close to the teacher?

Work in groups.

What you need:

① Pile the number blocks together.

② Ask your partner to name the positions of the numbers.

Example

1 is on **top**. 9 is at the **bottom**. 4 is **in front of** 3.

③ Switch roles and repeat ① and ②.

1 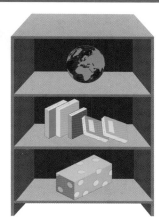 Compare using **top, middle** and **bottom**.

(a) The 🌐 is on the [   ] shelf.

(b) The 📚 are on the [   ] shelf.

(c) The 🎲 is on the [   ] shelf.

2 Describe using **on top of, in front of** and **above**.

(a) The pair of shoes is placed [   ] the pair of boots.

(b) One flip-flop is placed [   ] the other.

(c) The flip-flops are placed [   ] the pair of boots.

3 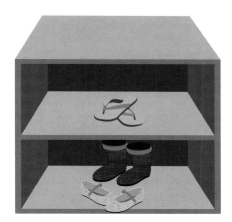 Describe using **around** and **near**.

(a) The trees are [   ] tree D.

(b) Tree E and tree G are [   ] tree H.

4 Fill in the blanks using **close to** and **far from**.

(a) England is [   ] Singapore.

(b) England is [   ] Scotland.

Complete Worksheet **1** – Page **143 – 144**

Describing Movements

In Focus

What is Amira doing?

Let's Learn

1

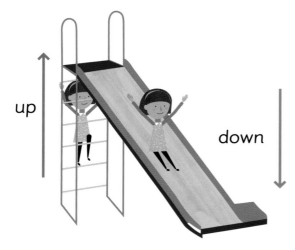

up

down

Amira climbs **up** the ladder.

Amira slides **down** the slide.

2

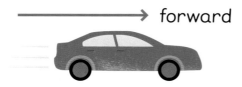 forward

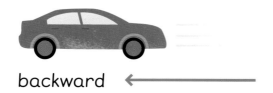 backward

The car went **forward**.

The car went **backward**.

3

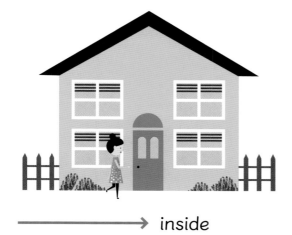

⟶ inside

Ruby went **inside** the house.

outside ⟵

Ruby went **outside** the house.

Activity Time

Play in groups of 3.

(1) You and your partner face each other.
The third pupil says **up, down, forward** or **backward**.

(2) You and your partner act out the word.

Example

up: jump

down: squat

forward: move one step forward

backward: move one step backward

(3) Whoever makes the wrong move 3 times loses the game and switches with the third pupil.

(4) Repeat (1) to (3).

Guided Practice

1 Describe using **up** and **down**.

(a) 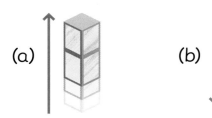 (b) (c) 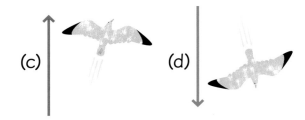 (d)

(a) The lift went ▢ .

(b) The lift went ▢ .

(c) The seagull flew ▢ .

(d) The seagull flew ▢ .

2 Describe using **forward** and **backward**.

 1, 2, 3, 4, 5, 6, 7, 8, 9

 9, 8, 7, 6, 5, 4, 3, 2, 1

Holly   Lulu

Holly is counting ▢ .

Lulu is counting ▢ .

3 Describe using **inside** and **outside**.

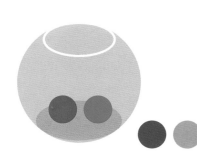

(a) The red ball is ▢ the bowl.

(b) The blue ball is ▢ the bowl.

(c) The orange ball is ▢ the bowl.

(d) The green ball is ▢ the bowl.

Complete Worksheet **2** – Page **145 – 146** ▶

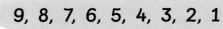

Making Turns

In Focus

Amira

Elliott

Ruby

Lulu

How do we describe different ways to turn our bodies?

Let's Learn

1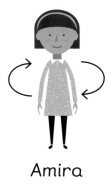

Amira made a **whole** turn.

> I remain on the same spot when making turns.

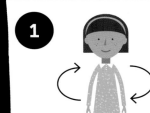

Elliott made a **half** turn.

Ruby made a **quarter** turn.

Lulu made a **three-quarter** turn.

> Is the turn clockwise or anticlockwise?

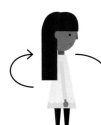

2

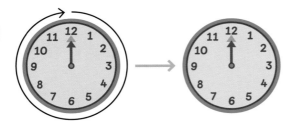

The hour hand made a whole turn.

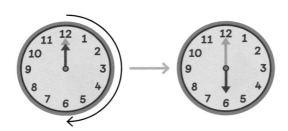

The hour hand made a half turn.

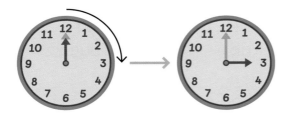

The hour hand made a quarter turn.

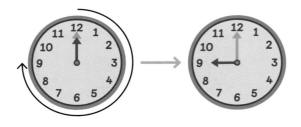

The hour hand made a
three-quarter turn.

Where will the hour hand be
if it makes 2 half turns?

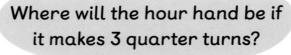

Where will the hour hand be if
it makes 3 quarter turns?

Play in groups of 3.

1. You and your partner face the same direction.
   The third pupil says **whole turn, half turn, quarter turn** or **three-quarter turn**.

2. You and your partner make the turn you are asked to.

3. The pupil who makes the wrong turn 3 times loses the game and switches with the third pupil.

4. Repeat ① to ③.

Guided Practice

Describe using **whole, half, quarter** and **three-quarter**.

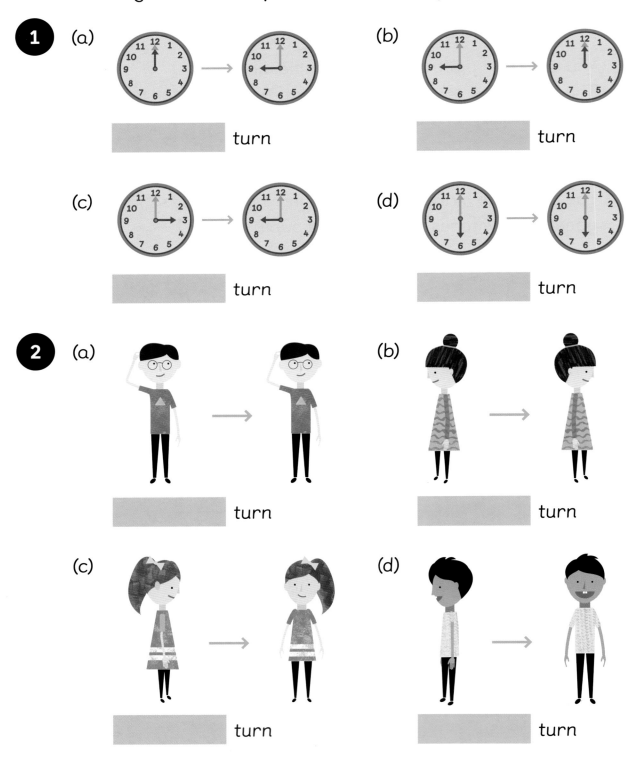

1 (a) _____ turn

(b) _____ turn

(c) _____ turn

(d) _____ turn

2 (a) _____ turn

(b) _____ turn

(c) _____ turn

(d) _____ turn

Complete Worksheet **3** – Page **147 – 148**

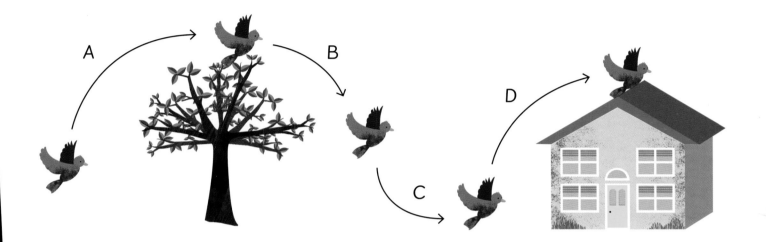

Describe the movement of the bird.

Example

The bird flew **up** and **forward** and stopped **on top of** a tree.

Stand up from your seat in class.

Choose someone in the class and write down in your journal the shortest directions to take to get to his or her seat.

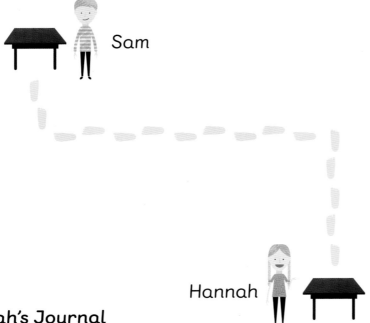

Hannah's Journal

I walked forward 5 steps, made a three-quarter turn clockwise, walked forward 9 steps, made a quarter turn clockwise and walked forward 2 steps to where Sam is.

I know how to...

☐ describe positions.

☐ describe movements.

☐ describe turns.

Self Check